Magical Animals

It DISAPPEARED!

Magical Animals
That Hide in
Plain Sight

by Nikki Potts

CAPSTONE PRESS
a capstone imprint

Thanks to our adviser for her expertise, research, and advice:
Jody Rake, Southwest Marine Educators Association

A+ Books are published by Capstone Press,
1710 Roe Crest Drive, North Mankato, Minnesota 56003
www.mycapstone.com

Library of Congress Cataloging-in-Publication Data
Library of Congress Cataloging-in-Publication Data is available
on the Library of Congress website.

ISBN: 978-1-5157-9465-3 (library hardcover) —
978-1-5157-9469-1 (paperback) — 978-1-5157-9473-8 (ebook)

Summary: A look at animals that camouflage themselves

Editorial Credits
Jaclyn Jaycox, editor; Ashlee Suker, designer;
Tracy Cummins, media researcher; Tori Abraham, production
specialist

Photo Credits
Alamy: National Geographic Creative/PRASENJEET YADAV,
16; Nature Picture Library: Yashpal Rathore, 17; Newscom:
David Chapman/NHPA/Photoshot, 18, Emanuele Biggi/
FLPA imageBROKER, 14; Shutterstock: Anna Veselova, 8,
AquariusPhotography, 13, chris2766, 28, Damian Herde, 24,
David Hicks, 2, 26, Florian Andronache, 19, ideation90, 27,
Jim Nelson, 11, John L. Absher, Back Cover, 29, Karen Faljyan,
22, Katarina Christenson, 25, Kjersti Joergensen, 12, Lori
Labrecque, 10, Marco Maggesi, 15, mastapiece, 1, 7, Matee
Nuserm, 6, reptiles4all, Cover, 9, Rich Carey, 20, 21, Teresa
Design Room, 23; Thinkstock: N.a. Planken-kooij, 4-5

Note to Parents, Teachers, and Librarians
This Magical Animals book uses full color photographs
and a nonfiction format to introduce the concept of animal
camouflage. *It Disappears* is designed to be read aloud to a
pre-reader or to be read independently by an early reader.
Photographs help listeners and early readers understand
the text and concepts discussed. The book encourages
further learning by including the following sections: Table of
Contents, Glossary, Read More, Internet Sites, Critical Thinking
Questions, and Index. Early readers may need assistance
using these features.

TABLE OF CONTENTS

4

Do you know what's watching you? Animals can be hidden all around us. They use camouflage to blend into their surroundings. A gecko can look like a leaf. An insect might look like a stick. Animals use camouflage to hide from predators. Some predators hide from prey until it's time to attack!

COMMON BARON
CATERPILLAR

Common baron caterpillars are found in India and Southeast Asia. They munch all day on mango tree leaves. This caterpillar has long, thin appendages. They look like the veins of a leaf. This bright green caterpillar blends in with the mango tree's leaves. A predator has a hard time spotting it among the leaves.

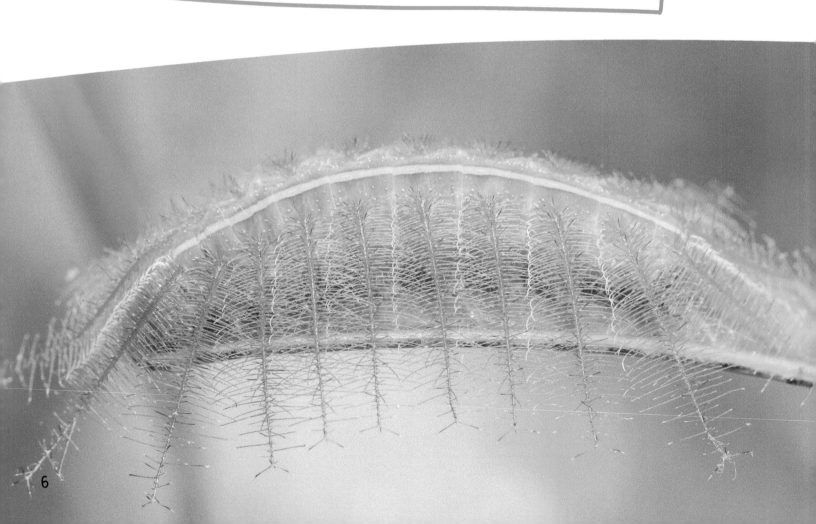

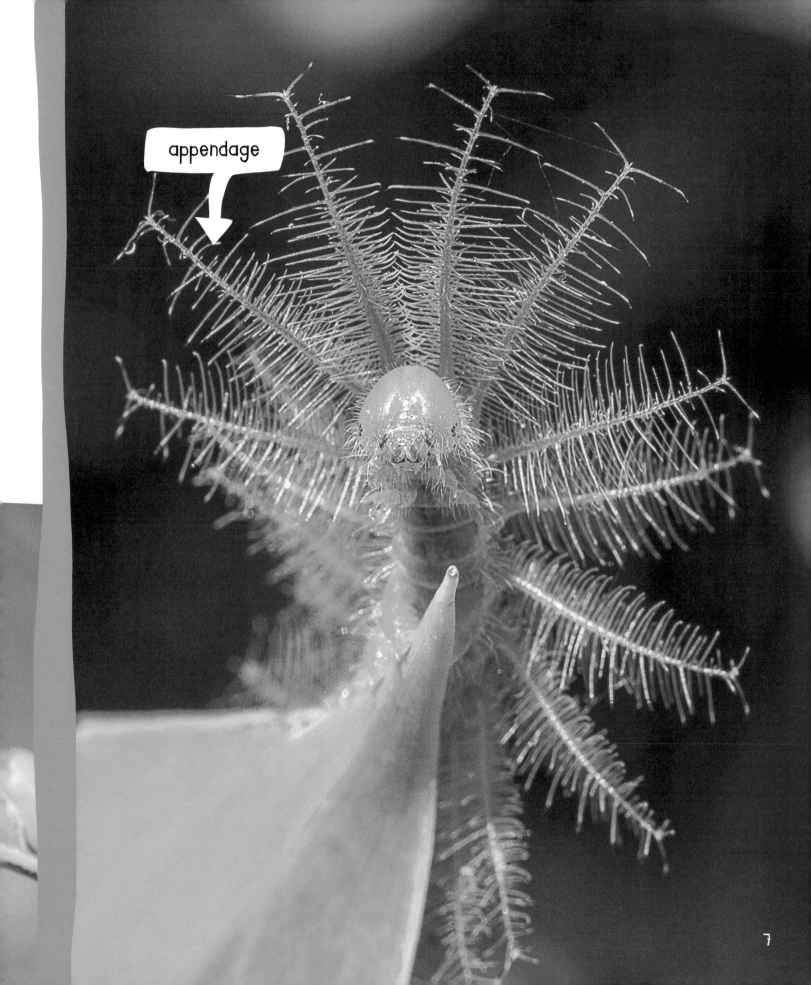

appendage

LEAF-TAILED GECKO

Leaf-tailed geckos are found on the island of Madagascar. They are brown and tan. A leaf-tailed gecko's tail looks like a dead leaf. This gecko twists its tail around its body during the day. It keeps very still among the leaves and branches. Snakes and birds can't spot the gecko. At night, the gecko comes out to hunt for bugs.

:: FUN FACT ::

Leaf-tailed geckos can live more than 10 years.

EASTERN SCREECH OWL

Eastern screech owls live east of the Rocky Mountains that span from Canada to New Mexico. They make their homes in many places. They can live in forests, parks, or cities. An Eastern screech owl's feathers look like tree bark. Sitting in a tree, this owl is tough to spot!

LEAFY SEA DRAGON

Leafy sea dragons are found off the coast of Australia. Most sea dragons are yellowish-green. A leafy sea dragon has many leaf-shaped limbs. The limbs help the animal blend in with seaweed and kelp. A small dorsal fin helps the sea dragon move through water. Leafy sea dragons swim very slowly. They can stay still for many hours.

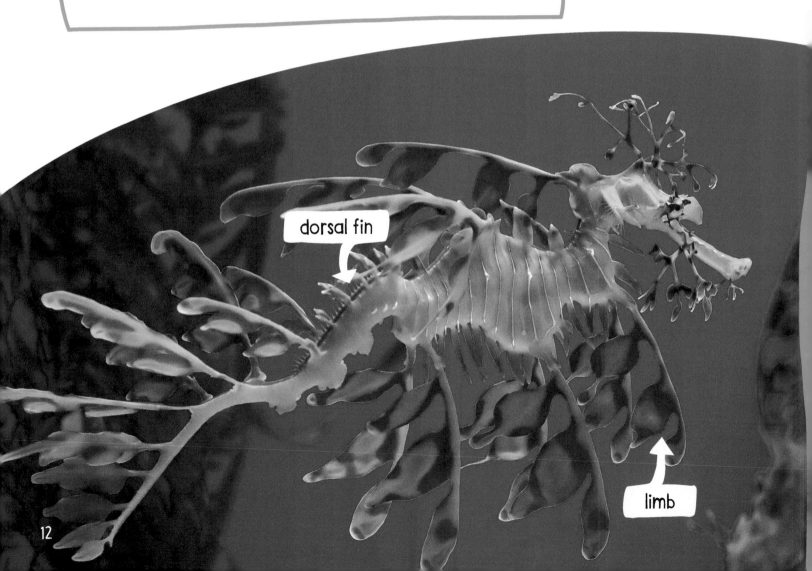

dorsal fin

limb

:: FUN FACT ::

Male leafy sea dragons care for the young. They carry the babies for four to six weeks.

TRAPDOOR SPIDER

The trapdoor spider doesn't camouflage itself. It makes a burrow and hides the door. The door is disguised to look like plants and soil. The spider hides inside. When prey comes near, the spider jumps out to catch it! Then the spider pulls its dinner into the burrow.

MALABAR FLYING FROG

Malabar flying frogs are found in the rain forests of India. Their bright green skin blends into the green leaves they perch on. A Malabar flying frog has webbed feet. The webbing helps it jump from tree to tree. It can leap 30–40 feet (9–12 meters)!

:: FUN FACT ::

The webbing between a Malabar flying frog's fingers and toes is orange-red.

ANGLE SHADES **MOTH**

An angle shades moth's wings are unique. Lines and patterns make the wings look like leaves. The green and brown wing colors help the moth hide among fall leaves. Predators can't see it!

SCORPIONFISH

Scorpionfish sit on the ocean floor among corals. There are more than 200 species of scorpionfish. Coral-colored skin flaps cover a scorpionfish's body. The color helps the scorpionfish hide in its surroundings. Scorpionfish are nocturnal. That means they rest during the day and hunt at night. They eat small fish, snails, and other crustaceans. A scorpionfish swallows prey whole with its wide, upturned mouth.

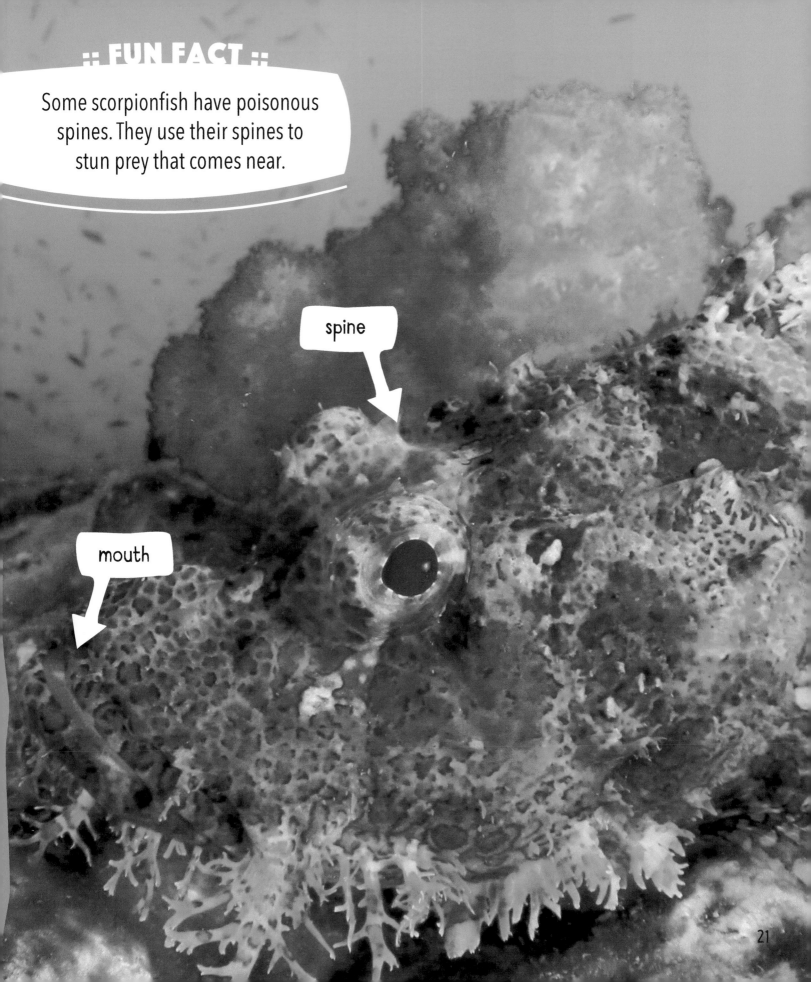

KATYDID

Katydids are found on every continent except Antarctica. They have long hind legs and antennae. Their green bodies look just like the green leaves they sit on. Hungry snakes, frogs, and birds can't see them. Katydids can reach more than 2 inches (5 centimeters) long. Katydids can't fly well, but they are great jumpers! They flutter their wings as they leap through the air.

:: FUN FACT ::

Male katydids attract mates by singing. They rub their wings together very fast to make sound.

WOLF SPIDER

Wolf spiders are found all around the world. With eight eyes, these spiders have excellent vision. Wolf spiders are very fast. They can run up to 2 feet (60 cm) per second. Some wolf spiders chase down their prey. Others stay still and surprise their prey. Wolf spiders can be brown, orange, tan, black, and gray. They depend on camouflage to keep them safe.

WALKING STICK

Walking sticks blend in with twigs and branches. They walk slowly on trees to look like a branch moving in the wind. Many species also play dead to avoid predators. Walking sticks live up to 3 years. They are usually brown. But some species are green or brightly colored. Most walking sticks are found in tropical climates.

OWL BUTTERFLY

Owl butterflies have huge eyespots on their wings. The eyespots look like the eyes of an owl. This resemblance is called mimicry. Some animals can look, sound, or smell like other animals in order to stay safe. The fake eyes scare birds and other predators away. Owl butterflies are found in the rain forests of Central America, South America, and Mexico.

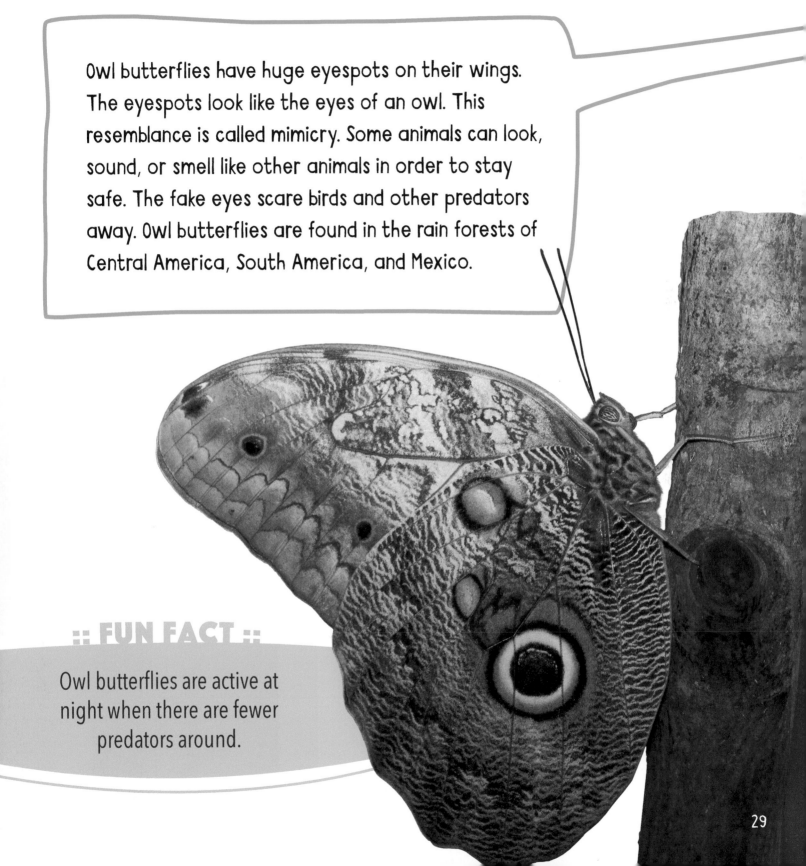

:: FUN FACT ::

Owl butterflies are active at night when there are fewer predators around.

GLOSSARY

ANTENNA—a feeler on an insect's head

APPENDAGE—a limb or other part that sticks out of an animal or plant

BARK—hard covering of a tree

BURROW—a hole in the ground made or used by an animal

CAMOUFLAGE—a pattern or color on an animal's skin that helps it blend in with the things around it

CONTINENT—one of Earth's seven large land masses

CRUSTACEAN—a sea animal with an outer skeleton, such as a crab, lobster, or shrimp

DORSAL FIN—a fin located on the back

KELP—a large, brown seaweed

MATE—the male or female partner of a pair of animals

NOCTURNAL—active at night and resting during the day

PERCH—to stand on the edge of something

PREY—an animal hunted by another animal for food

SPECIES—a group of animals with similar features

SURROUNDINGS—the things around something or someone

TROPICAL CLIMATE—weather that is warm and rainy

UNIQUE—one of a kind

VEIN—one of the stiff, narrow tubes that form the framework of a leaf

VISION—sight

Read MORE

Belback, Elsie. *Hidden in Plain Sight: Animal Camouflage.* Close-Up on Amazing Animals. North Mankato, Minn.: Rourke Educational Media, 2015.

Peterson, Megan Cooley. *The Best Camouflaged Animals.* Extreme Animals. North Mankato, Minn.: Capstone Press, 2012.

Royston, Angela. *Animals that Hide.* Adapted to Survive. Chicago: Capstone Raintree, 2014.

Internet SITES

Use FactHound to find Internet sites related to this book.

Visit www.facthound.com

Just type in 9781515794653 and go.

Check out projects, games and lots more at
www.capstonekids.com

Critical Thinking QUESTIONS

1. Where can you find Malabar flying frogs?

2. Scorpionfish are nocturnal. What does this mean?
   Hint: Use your glossary for help!

3. Which of the animals in this book is your favorite? Why?

::INDEX::